IMAGES
of America

ONONDAGA COUNTY
SHERIFF'S OFFICE

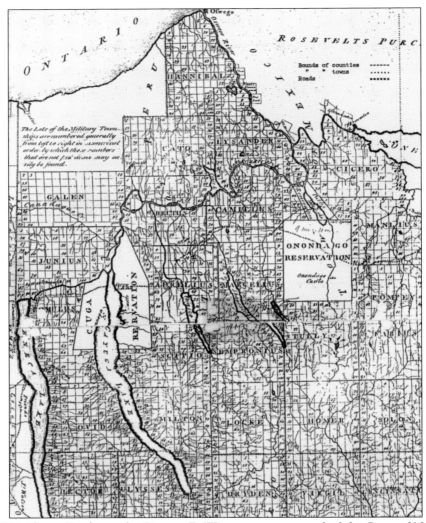

This 1792 *Military Track* map by Simeon DeWitt, surveyor general of the State of New York, illustrates the extent of land that comprised Onondaga County when it was formed on March 5, 1794. This tract contained land grants to veterans of the Revolutionary War. The new county covered 1.75 million acres and included all of what is today Onondaga, Cortland, and Seneca Counties and parts of Oswego, Tompkins, Schuyler, Yates, Wayne, Tioga, and Herkimer Counties. The county would eventually be reduced to an 800-square-mile territory by 1848. (Courtesy of the Onondaga County Sheriff's Office.)

ON THE COVER: By 1970, the Onondaga County Sheriff's Office maintained a special service section that provided specialty units to augment law-enforcement patrols. The section utilized boat, motorcycle, and snowmobile patrols. Specialty units would continue to be developed into operation. These would come to include an aviation-helicopter unit, a dive team, explosive ordnance team, traffic accident–investigation team, SWAT, K-9 units, and crime scene specialists. Pictured here in 1970 are Deputy Paul Stevenson, in the boat, and from left to right on motorcycles are Michael Carbery, Robert Bowles, J.J. Coyne, and Thomas Stark. (Courtesy of the Onondaga County Sheriff's Office.)

IMAGES
of America

ONONDAGA COUNTY
SHERIFF'S OFFICE

Jonathan L. Anderson

Mike
With compliments
Jon

ARCADIA
PUBLISHING

Published by Arcadia Publishing
Charleston, South Carolina

Printed in the United States of America

Library of Congress Control Number: 2015939112

For all general information, please contact Arcadia Publishing:
Telephone 843-853-2070
Fax 843-853-0044
E-mail sales@arcadiapublishing.com
For customer service and orders:
Toll-Free 1-888-313-2665

Visit us on the Internet at www.arcadiapublishing.com

This book is dedicated to the men and women of the Onondaga County Sheriff's Office; past, present, and future.

CONTENTS

ACKNOWLEDGMENTS

Sincere appreciation is expressed to the past membership and families of the Onondaga County Sheriff's Office for the many contributions to the office's historical preservation initiative.

Unless otherwise noted, all of the photographic images presented are courtesy of the Onondaga County Sheriff's Office historic preservation archives.

Passionate appreciation is deserving of the best backup I have ever experienced or could have ever imagined and hoped for: my wife, Patti.

INTRODUCTION

In 1994, the late sheriff John C. Dillon wrote the following about the Onondaga County Sheriff's Office for the bicentennial:

> For two hundred years, the Sheriff has served as the chief law enforcement officer of Onondaga County with dignity and professionalism. During that time, the office of the Sheriff grew and expanded in size and ability to meet the law enforcement needs of the residents.
>
> Today, the Onondaga County Sheriff's Department is considered a leader among law enforcement agencies in the state and has become a role model for others to follow in the field of training, equipment, and technology.
>
> I am proud to serve as the 59th Sheriff of Onondaga County and I am fortunate to have the opportunity to reflect on the accomplishments of the past and look ahead to the growth and progress of the future.
>
> As we approach the beginning of the twenty first century, I am hopeful that some of the problems that have plagued our community will soon be solved. Poverty, unemployment, crime and racism are ugly reminders of our failures of the past.
>
> Through hard work, understanding and education, we can correct the problems of the past and present and enjoy a future in Onondaga County where our children and grandchildren will be safe, healthy and prosperous.

The Onondaga County Sheriff's Office of today is made up of more than 650 police, custody, and civil-department members, special deputies, and civilian support staff. The office serves an 827-square-mile county with a population of more than half a million people. The sheriff's office serves a community encompassing the city of Syracuse, 19 towns, 15 villages, and a Native American (Haudenosaunee, Onondaga Nation) reservation territory. Throughout its history, the office has continually adapted to answer the demands of the diverse community it serves.

Despite the longevity of the Onondaga County Sheriff's Office, it was surprising to find, upon the advent of the agency's 1994 bicentennial, that much of its recorded history was lost and uncelebrated. True to the demands of the profession, the office had focused attention upon current and future needs, and very little attention was directed toward recovering, preserving, and promoting its professional heritage.

Inspired by the bicentennial, the office initiated an investigative effort targeted at researching and promoting its history. It was evident at the onset that recovering a 200-year organizational history from scratch was a formidable task. It was as if that history had been written upon a chalkboard, and each passing era's history was partly erased and overwritten by succeeding generations. What were left were historical sketches, of what should have been a full portrait.

As the project progressed, a network of professional, community, historical, and educational resources emerged that shared historical interests. Tapping into these resources promoted local and national publications and a variety of professional-training initiatives. Further, the project promoted a wide range of community-related programs and events that offered innovative opportunities for the office to capture the attention and interest of the public and promote better understanding of the contribution and interactive link that the office had upon the community throughout local history.

The effort became a focal point from which to reconnect with the agency's extended retired membership and their families. Their scrapbooks, memorabilia, and interviews provided personal character to the overall endeavor. Recognizing the contributions of previous generations produced an inspirational sense of accomplishment and shared fraternal pride amongst the office membership. This served as an integral ingredient for fostering a sense of professionalism.

The historical initiative proved rewarding beyond all expectations. It resulted in the creation of an extensive historical research and photographic file, a significant historical artifact collection, the adoption of an official slogan, "Since 1794," numerous historic celebrative initiatives, posthumous award recognitions, the adoption of a 2000 millennium badge, and the adoption of a formal historian position.

One iconic message revealed by the initiative reflected back to the March 5, 1794, formation of the office. At that time, its jurisdiction covered what was previously known as the Military Track, a 1.75-million-acre tract of land made available as bounty to soldiers of the Continental army during the Revolutionary War. As such, the founding fathers of the sheriff's office, veterans of that epic conflict, suffered and fought for the very ideals that bore the oath that sheriff's office members would recite upon taking office for generations to come.

Every law enforcement and correctional officer senses it, and every officer is indebted to it; it is the spirit of legacy that is woven into the professional tapestry of the past, the present, and the future. That legacy forever harmonizes the generations that were, are, and are yet to follow.

It is a privilege to have this opportunity to share this history of the Onondaga County Sheriff's Office through Arcadia Publishing's Images of America series.

—Lt. Jonathan L. Anderson
Historian, Onondaga County Sheriff's Office

Pictured here is the author, Lt. Jon L. Anderson, in his formal service uniform.

The sheriff's office historical collection maintains a number of vintage badges extending from 1900 to 2015. Prior to the 1940s, badges were silver, gold, or a combination of those two metallic colors. In the 1940s, colored enamel began to adorn badge details.

One

THE OFFICE OF THE SHERIFF

Early origins of the sheriff title evolved in England during the Anglo-Saxon and Norman Common Law periods. During these eras, the sheriff duties included apprehending offenders, maintaining jail facilities, carrying out writs of the courts, and mobilizing civil force in cases of emergency. During these periods, the law enforcer of a shire (comparable to a county jurisdiction) was known as the reeve (keeper). It was from this title and responsibility that the term sheriff derived; from shire (county) and reeve (keeper), to shire-reeve (the county's keeper), to sheriff.

Since the legal system in the United States developed along English common law lines, it maintained the position of sheriff and the traditions that accompany that position. These traditions allow the office of the sheriff to occupy a unique place in the justice system, serving civil process, maintaining jail facilities, and providing law-enforcement services.

SHERIFFS OF ONONDAGA COUNTY

1794	John Harris	1876	John J. Meldram
1796	Abaither Hull	1879	Hiram K. Edwards
1797	Comfort Tyler	1882	Minor G. Bennett
1799	Elnathan Beach	1885	Thomas R. O'Neil
1801	Ebenezer R. Hawley	1888	Hector B. Johnson
1804	Elijah Phillips	1891	John A. Hoxie
1808	Robert Earll	1894	Oscar F. Austin
1810	Elijah Rust	1897	Stephen Thornton
1811	Robert Earll	1901	Charles W. Marvin
1813	Elijah Rust	1904	William H. Turner
1815	Jonas Earll (February 28)	1906	Thomas F. Walsh
1819	Hezekiah L. Granger (February 9)	1910	Fred Wyker
1819	Giles Cornish (June 9)	1912	John H. Cahill
1821	Luther Marsh	1913	James F. Mathews
1825	Lewis Smith	1916	John P. Schlosser
1828	John H. Johnson	1918	Edward G. TenEyck
1831	Johnson Hall	1922	Isaac C. Davis
1834	Dorastus Lawrence	1926	Lewis C. Scriber
1837	Elihu L. Phillips	1928	Michael W. O'Brien
1840	Frederick Benson	1930	John Sleeth
1844	Heber Weatherby	1934	Thomas Munro
1846	Joshua C. Cuddeback	1937	Edwin R. Auer
1849	William C. Gardner	1942	Charles R. Tindall
1852	Holland W. Chadwick		(Died June 23, 1943)
1855	James M. Munroe	1943	Robert G. Wasmer
1858	George L. Maynard	1953	Albert E. Stone (Died October 1959)
1861	Byron D. Benson	1959	Sarto C. Major
1864	Jared C. Williams	1964	Patrick J. Corbett
1867	Dewitt C. Toll	1978	John C. Dillon
1870	William Evans	1995	Kevin E. Walsh
1873	David Cossitt	2015	Eugene J. Conway

This gravestone of Col. John Harris, Onondaga County's first sheriff (1794–1796) is located on the west side of Owasco Lake, in Auburn, New York. Early 19th-century sheriffs were appointed by the state governor and paid by a fee system for services rendered, including transporting prisoners, making arrests, and serving civil process. The office became an elected and salaried post in 1846. Terms of office for sheriffs were limited to four-year terms until 1938.

Comfort Tyler served as sheriff from 1797 to 1798. Tyler was a Revolutionary War veteran and a prominent personality during the early settlement period of the county. He settled in the Military Tract (Onondaga County 1794) in 1788. He served as a postmaster, teacher, surveyor, justice of the peace, coroner, town supervisor, and the first salt manufacturer at Onondaga Lake. Tyler was a favorite among the native people, who called him To-Whau-Tague, which means "one that is double," being both a laboring man and a gentleman. He is buried in Oakwood Cemetery in Syracuse, New York.

Comfort Tyler...

Hiram K. Edwards served as sheriff from 1879 to 1881. Edwards was the last sheriff of Onondaga County to serve as hangman for a legal execution by gallows: the August 5, 1881, execution of Nathan Orlando Greenfield for the murder of his spouse, Alice Bloodgood Greenfield, in Orwell Oswego County. Oswego County suffered two mistrials in the murder trial. As a result, the trial was moved to Onondaga County, where a conviction was rendered. Edwards vowed never to hang another man. Holding to that vow, he would never seek another term as sheriff.

Charles W. Marvin served as sheriff from 1901 to 1904. The era of the new century brought an exodus of the state's population from rural to urban settings. Prior to 1900, four out of five New Yorkers lived on farms or in smaller villages. Between 1800 and 1900, the state population rose from 600,000 to 7.2 million. By 1900, some 70 percent of the state's population was urban. New challenges faced law enforcement and correctional authorities across the state. In Onondaga County, a new Jamesville Penitentiary opened on April 15, 1901, and housed all penitentiary and jail prisoners.

William H. Turner served as sheriff from 1904 to 1905. A September 8, 1914, county board of supervisor's journal referenced Turner's death: "Whereas it has pleased Almighty God to remove from this community, after a life of good usefulness, both as a private citizen and as a useful public official . . . Resolved, that we . . . the board of supervisors of Onondaga County, do hereby publicly express our deep sorrow upon the demise of Mr. Turner and do hereby extend to the members of his family and a large circle of sorrowing friends, our most sincere and heartfelt sympathy."

James Mathews served as sheriff from 1913 to 1915. In 1914, the sheriff's annual salary amounted to $4,000. A deputy's annual salary amounted to $900. Monthly office compensations included groceries, ice, swing services, livery hire, Western Union Telegraph charges, and other miscellaneous services amounting to about $1,400. The monthly cost of maintaining the jail was claimed on a combined penitentiary-jail fund. This included groceries, hardware, tobacco, insurance, drugs, lumber, leather items, coal, oil, and photographic services amounting to about $5,500.

This photograph of Sheriff Thomas Munro was featured in his obituary in the *Marcellus Observer* on February 23, 1939. Thomas Munro served as sheriff from 1934 to 1937. Sheriff Munro equipped the patrol-fleet motorcycles with one-way radios in 1936. These police motorcycle and prowl cars patrolled the county roads in hunt for speeders and reckless drivers and conducted accident investigations. At the time of his death, Munro was vice president of the NYS Sheriff's Association. He is buried in the family plot in Maplewood Cemetery in Camillus, New York.

Edwin R. Auer served as sheriff from 1937 to 1942. In 1938, it became legal for a sheriff to be elected for successive terms. Sheriff Auer appointed three women deputy sheriffs to assist women jurors and handle civil and criminal work. Renovations to the Cedar Street jail included escape-proof electrically controlled cell locks. In 1939, a dramatic prisoner transport escape attempt made by six Attica Prison convicts was thwarted when Deputy Lester Rawlings fatally shot one of the convicts in a struggle for the deputy's holstered weapon.

Charles R. Tindall served as sheriff from 1942 to 1943. Tindall's term of office was unfortunately short-lived due to his untimely death in mid-1943. He was evidently admired by his deputies, for they presented him with a personalized badge complete with several inlaid precious stones and inscribed "Presented to Sheriff Charles R. Tindall by his deputies and friends, March 17, 1943." Tindall died three months later.

Robert Wasmer served as sheriff from 1943 to 1952. Following the death in office of Sheriff Charles Tindall, Governor Dewey appointed Wasmer as sheriff on June 32, 1943. He was elected sheriff the following year.

Albert Stone, pictured here on June 7, 1952, served as sheriff from 1953 to 1959. Stone was appointed undersheriff in 1945 under Sheriff Robert Wasmer. He was elected to the office of sheriff in 1953. Sheriff Stone died in office in October 1959. Nearly 1,000 people jammed St. Paul's Episcopal Church for his funeral. He is buried in Woodlawn Cemetery.

Sarto C. Major served as sheriff from 1959 to 1963. Major assumed office by appointment in 1959 when Sheriff Albert E. Stone died in office in October of that year. Major was elected sheriff the following year 1960. During this administration, the six-point star badge pattern was adopted by sheriff offices across New York State. Sheriff Major took a visible role in improving and consolidating police training programs and toward advocating improvements in jail facility development.

Patrick J. Corbett served as sheriff from 1964 to 1977. Corbett organized the agency into a department with three (police, jail, and civil) divisions. The department cohabitated the Public Safety Building with the City of Syracuse Police and Fire Departments. This term was hallmarked by developments in academy training, civil service–hiring process, specialized enforcement units such as boat, scuba, snowmobile, motorcycle, unmarked vehicle radar patrols, SWAT., and the helicopter aviation program, and improved county-wide police radio-communication system.

John C. Dillon, pictured here around 1985, served as sheriff from 1978 to 1994. Dillon's term highlights included establishing operational relations with the Onondaga Nation Reservation Territory, achieving accreditation standards, improving the telecommunication system, implementing the criminal history arrest incident reporting system (CHAIRS), computerizing E-911 dispatch, a fingerprint-identification system, improving specialized enforcement units, utilizing of substation facilities, and developments toward securing an improved jail facility—Onondaga County Justice Center.

Kevin E. Walsh served as sheriff from 1995 to 2014. Sheriff Walsh held the longest term of office in Onondaga County. Term hallmarks included the opening of the direct supervision Justice Center Jail, reorganizing the agency into an office with three (police, custody, civil) departments, consolidation efforts in crime lab-scene and special-victim investigations and services, technological developments in patrol vehicle reporting systems, improved informational-management system, and improved substation facilities.

Garnished with green carnations, Sheriff Eugene J. Conway (front center) is pictured with members of the sheriff's office at the 2015 St. Patrick's Day parade. Conway was elected Onondaga County Sheriff for the 2015 term. (Courtesy of RC Photo Designs.)

The sheriff's office historical collection maintains uniform items for display or uniform-presentation details. Original vintage uniforms have been incorporated into funeral, parade, and award-ceremony details. Pictured here are 1869 handcuffs (left), a truncheon baton from about 1900, a whistle and chain from about 1944, a 1944 badge, an eight-point police cap from between 1944 and 1964, and an 1851 handcuff.

Two

In the Line of Duty

There have been 17 law enforcement officers who have lost their lives in the line of duty throughout Onondaga County's history:

July 31, 1893	Syracuse Police officer James Harvey
April 20, 1907	Madison County undersheriff Michael Mooney
June 12, 1921	Syracuse Police officer Ernest Griffin
January 6, 1921	Syracuse Police officer Peirson Near
July 10, 1928	Syracuse Police officer George Caldwell
May 1, 1929	Syracuse Police officer James Hannon
September 22, 1935	Syracuse Police officer Michael English
February 1, 1937	Syracuse Police officer Andrew Wolsrom
July 29, 1941	New York State trooper Robert Moore
August 30, 1947	Syracuse Police officer John Jarmacz
April 7, 1954	Syracuse Police officer James Considine
September 23, 1954	Syracuse Police officer Mercer Weiskotten
October 24, 1974	New York State trooper Emerson Dillon
February 10, 1987	Onondaga County sheriff deputy David Clark
October 30, 1990	Syracuse Police officer Wallie Howard Jr.
November 29, 2003	Onondaga County sheriff deputy Glenn M. Searles
April 23, 2006	New York State trooper Craig J. Todeschini

Pictured is the February 1987 funeral for jail division deputy David Clark at Assumption Church. On February 10, 1987, Deputy Bernard Meleski and Deputy David Clark suffered gunshot injuries thwarting a failed escape attempt during a prisoner transport at the Town of Dewitt Court. Prisoner William Blake stole the holstered weapon of Deputy Meleski and fired upon the deputies. Blake was apprehended in the parking lot of the courthouse. Clark died several hours later as a result of his injury.

Piper Scott Anderson and the City of Syracuse Police Department honor guard are pictured in this December 4, 2003, funeral service for Deputy Glenn Searles. The tune playing when this photograph was taken was "When the Battle Is Over."

Onondaga County sheriff deputy Glenn M. Searles is pictured here in 2001. Deputy Searles was killed in the line of duty on November 29, 2003.

Pictured here is the marker etching of Glenn M. Searles from the National Law Enforcement Officers Memorial in Washington, DC. On November 29, 2003, Onondaga County sheriff deputy Glenn Searles was killed by a passing vehicle during a disabled-vehicle call on Route 481 to Dewitt. The incident was one of two similar incidents that led to New York State's move-over law signed and put into law effective January 1, 2011. The law was named for New York State trooper Robert W. Ambrose and Onondaga County deputy Glenn Searles.

In 1994, the "Since 1794" slogan was adopted in celebration of the agency's bicentennial. The slogan was later added to a red banner and attached to the agency seven-point patch insignia.

Three

THE JAILS

One of the intriguing theaters of the sheriff's office legacy is the management of the county's jail facilities. Since the early 1800s, the county has maintained five jail and three penitentiary facilities. The sheriff's responsibility has focused on maintaining the jails whereas superintendents have managed the penitentiaries. The early jails housed debtors and criminals. Both the jails and penitentiaries served as 18th-century execution grounds, the sheriff acting as hangman.

The 20th century witnessed many changes in societal views of the criminal and the incarcerated, trends in crime, and the evolution of jail construction, management, and jail-penitentiary consolidation strategies. The jails have and will continue to enact an important role toward meeting the demands of the criminal-justice system and community security–public safety needs.

ONONDAGA HILL
JAIL
1802 - 1829

Construction for the county's first jail, or gaol, on Onondaga Hill began in 1802 and was completed in 1810. The first floor of the jail housed cells and an apartment for the jailer. The second floor served as a courthouse. The cells were of heavy oak plank, fastened with wrought-iron spikes. A diamond-shaped hole was cut in the center of the cell doors to pass the food and light to the prisoners. Grated windows adorned the rear of the cells. Criminals and debtors were held at the jail. The first jailbreak occurred from this jail in 1812, involving the escape of several debtors. The structure was replaced by a new jail in 1929.

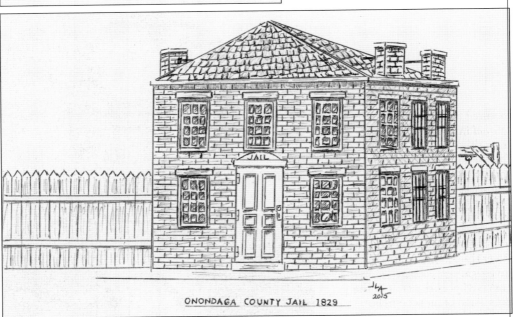

ONONDAGA COUNTY JAIL 1829

The county's second jail was located on the corner of Ash Street and Division Street in Syracuse. The jail served as the gallows site for the county's first (nonpublic) legal execution on November 19, 1840. Zachariah Freeman Jr. was executed by Sheriff Elihu Philips. According to an April 18, 1873, *Syracuse Courier* article, a large crowd gathered for the execution, and so great was their excitement that it was with difficulty that they were kept from breaking down a tall stockade fence erected around the jail execution yard. A county penitentiary replaced this jail in 1850.

ONONDAGA COUNTY PENITENTIARY mid-19th C.

Onondaga County's first penitentiary opened about 1850. The facility served as a penitentiary and jail under the control and management of a superintendent. The site served as the gallows site for three Onondaga County legal executions, April 18, 1873, February 11, 1876, and August 5, 1881. On each of those occasions, the sheriff of Onondaga County acted as hangman. The penitentiary was replaced by a new Jamesville Penitentiary in 1901.

Pictured here is a *Syracuse Daily Journal* image of Owen Lindsay from February 11, 1876. On that day, Lindsay was executed by Sheriff Davis Cossitt for the murder of Francis A. Colvin. The murder took place in December 1873 over the want of Colvin's pocket watch. Colvin's body was discovered in the Seneca River the following June. The investigation recovered Colvin's engraved pocket watch in the possession of an accomplice Bishop Varder. Lindsay was executed by a famous gallows known as the galloping gallows, a device that lifted its victim up from the neck by the drop of a counterweight.

The Cedar Street Jail opened about 1917. This photograph dates to about 1925. Some references indicate that the building's use as a jail was modified or limited in 1946. In April 1957, the sheriff's office's criminal division moved its headquarters from the county court house to the Cedar Street Jail. The jail closed in 1964 when it was replaced by the Public Safety Building Jail. That facility operated from 1964 to 1994. In 2000, the Public Safety Building was dedicated to the late Patrick J. Corbett (sheriff 1964–1977).

The Onondaga County Justice Center Jail, a direct-supervision facility with 616 beds, opened in 1995.

Four

VEHICLES AND SPECIAL ENFORCEMENT

The introduction of the automobile has proven to be one of the most dynamic and iconic developments in policing. It mobilized policing toward meeting the ever-changing trends in crime, technology, law-enforcement strategies, and public demands for safety and security. The adaptation of the motor vehicle for police work has evolved it into a practicable and visible sophisticated mobile crime-fighting unit.

Specialized enforcement units for addressing seasonal, terrain, and waterway challenges served as practical means for augmenting primary law-enforcement functions. The introduction of the helicopter in 1975 added an innovative strategy for serving the combined law enforcement, emergency medical service, and firefighting first responder force.

This 1928 photograph of the sheriff's office first motorcycle patrol features 1927 model Harley Davidson motorcycles, without front brakes. Front brakes were added the following year. These early cycles boasted about 20 horsepower. They featured a throttle-controlled engine-oiling system and a chassis-lubrication system that allowed the bike to be completely greased in only a few minutes. They also featured a weatherproof and waterproof ignition system. A patented cushion seat with a post and spring arrangement offered a comfortable perch.

Deputy Harold Griebno is pictured here around 1936. The sheriff's office utilized motorcycle patrols from 1928 to 1980. Until the introduction of the two-way radio, motorcycle patrols were required to make regular status checks at pole-mounted call boxes throughout their tour. The motorcycle was discontinued for county policing, as the automobile proved to be safer, more practical, and less expensive to maintain.

Syracuse Herald-Journal

1937 jail transport wagon.

Pictured here is a *Syracuse Herald Journal* image of the Onondaga County Sheriff's Office jail transport wagon from 1937.

Pictured here in the 1940s are, from left to right, Deputy Harold Griebno, Deputy Sylvester Eslick, and an unidentified NYS trooper.

Deputy Harold Griebno (right) is pictured here around 1940 directing traffic. In 1937, the sheriff's office reported 53 traffic fatalities in the county. The following year, the number of reported traffic fatalities was 46.

Deputy Bert Reardon (right) and an unidentified fellow officer are pictured here in the 1940s.

Pictured here in the 1940s is a motorcycle parade escort. Deputy Bert Reardon is identified on the right. The deputy on the left is unidentified.

Pictured here on Sunday, August 22, 1948, are John Joy, Floyd Cisco, Bert Reardon, Joseph DeMore, Henry Coughlin, Sylvester Eslick, and John Checkowski.

Pictured here by the Cedar Street Jail in 1948 are, from left to right, deputies John Checkowski, Herald Griebno, Vick Tucci, and Dewitt Cummings.

This c. 1948 photograph of Deputy John Head is a curious one. Although the uniform dates to the late 1940s, the illustrated badge (gold) dated to a previous era, the mid-to-late 1930s. It is known that Deputy Head retired in 1970 after 22 years of service. It is speculated that he donned an early badge in the photograph when newly appointed, perhaps due to the unavailability of updated badges.

Deputy Bert Reardon is pictured here in the 1950s.

This photograph is dated 1953. New recruits during this time were trained during a two-week session at the county jail. This school was part of a long-range policing-training program instituted in 1945 in New York State. The program was jointly sponsored by the New York State Sheriff's Association, the State Association of Chiefs of Police, and the FBI. The sheriff's office rosters of the era hovered around 200 members, supplemented by varying numbers of special deputies.

This photograph of Deputy Bert Reardon is dated June 29, 1957. By 1954, four local police officers in Onondaga County (four City of Syracuse Police officers, and one NYS trooper) had been killed as a result of motorcycle accidents. By 1957, the sheriff's office began to employ helmets for their motorcycle-patrol officers.

This photograph dated October 17, 1958, shows a sheriff-marked vehicle crash on Route 81 near Nedrow.

Deputy Floyd Harrison (center left) and Sgt. Blanchard Crysler (right) stop for a coffee break in 1959.

Pictured here in 1959 are unidentified members of the sheriff's department. That year, the sheriff's office roster listed 210 members, 10 special deputies, and 14 others assigned to security posts at Syracuse transit, City of Syracuse Parks Department, Onondaga County Court House, Crouse Hinds, Bristol Co., Suburban Park, Hub City, Crucible Steel, and the Jamesville Penitentiary.

On June 29, 1959, the sheriff's office investigated a fatal car-pedestrian accident on Dave Tilden Road in Jamesville.

Pictured here on October 7, 1957, is a marked OCSO Pontiac Catalina. In April of that year, the sheriff office's criminal division moved from the county courthouse to the Cedar Street Jail building. The civil division remained at the courthouse.

These motorcycle patrolmen are pictured on June 5, 1960. From left to right are Theodore Marsh, William Hayford, Joseph DeMore, Bruce Shattuck, unidentified, and Sheriff Sarto C. Major (standing).

By August 1961, the sheriff's office recorded 57 traffic deaths across the county.

Pictured here is OSCO's motorcycle patrol around 1960–1961.

Scrapbooks from retired members of the sheriff's office provide valuable images. Deputy James Sauer is pictured here around 1962.

Lt. Anthony Valleriani is pictured here around 1962.

In the early 1960s, the sheriff's motorcycle patrol adopted a powder blue uniform top, worn here by Deputy James Sauer.

This photograph from about 1962 features motorcycle patrol deputy James Sauer.

This photograph dated May 25, 1966, shows a motorcycle parade escort.

Deputy Jerry Harrington is pictured here in the mid-1960s.

Between 1960 and 1964, the sheriff's department utilized an armored vehicle for special operations.

On June 15, 1962, the sheriff's office investigated a fatal vehicle crash on Rock Cut Road in the town of Onondaga.

This photograph is related to a fatal vehicle crash on September 10, 1963, investigated at the intersection of Routes 31 and 173 in the town of Vanburen. Among the many questions listed on period traffic reports were How many years has a driver been driving? How many miles per year does the driver drive per year? Has the driver been involved in any previous accidents? If so, how many?

The parade color guard pictured here around 1967 depicts the uniform style of the Onondaga County Sheriff's Office. Pictured here are, from left to right, deputies Thomas Lavere, J.J. Coyne, and unidentified.

During the mid-1960s, the sheriff's department utilized the Dodge Plymouth Fury for its patrol fleet.

On August 16, 1967, squads of 12-man three-car caravans were organized to respond to a three-day civil disturbance that erupted in the lower east side of the city of Syracuse. Bands of as many as 200 area youths rampaged the neighborhood, starting fires, looting, opening fire hydrants, and smashing the windows of vehicles and businesses. Sheriff Patrick Corbett declared a special emergency and assumed command of a multicounty mutual-aid response plan in suppressing the disturbance. The power play restraint by law enforcement was cited for the successful containment of the situation.

Pictured here in the 1970s is a tank escort detail. The circumstance of the escort is unknown. The detail was most likely a parade or military-maneuver escort detail.

By 1970, the sheriff's department had organized a special service section. On the foot-shifted shovelhead motorcycles are, from left to right, Michael Carbery, Robert Bowles, J.J. Coyne, Thomas Stark, Sam Fischera, and Daniel Stauffer. Pictured in the patrol boat are, from left to right, William Stonecipher and Paul Stevenson; standing left to right are Sheriff Patrick Corbett, Undersheriff Robert Alexander, and Capt. Blanchard Crysler.

In 1964, Sheriff Corbett introduced a county-wide police radio network titled the Onondaga Law Enforcement Mobile Radio District (OLMRD). Pictured here is Deputy Richard Flanagan Sr.

A 911-dispatch system idea was introduced as early as 1971 in Onondaga County. However, that would not become a reality until 1992. Deputy Mike Harrington is pictured here.

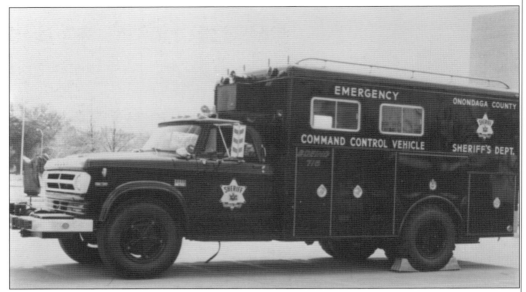

In 1964, the Onondaga County Sheriff's Office included an emergency command control vehicle in its fleet.

In the mid-1970s, the sheriff's office utilized snowmobiles for specialized patrol operations. Onondaga County Sheriff's Office was the first law enforcement agency in the county to utilize the roof-mounted light bar for patrol vehicles. This image is dated January 26, 1975.

Pictured here in 1975 are code red lights and a patrol vehicle emergency response. The Onondaga County Sheriff's Office was the first police agency in the county to equip its marked patrol vehicles with the roof bar-light system. With the introduction of a helicopter aviation program in 1975, patrol car roofs were marked with identification numbers for aerial observation.

By 1975, blood transports, or blood runs, from the Red Cross Regional Blood Center in Syracuse were undertaken by patrol units to the county line for pick up by deputies from neighboring counties. This service provided delivery of blood to hospitals in a 15-county region.

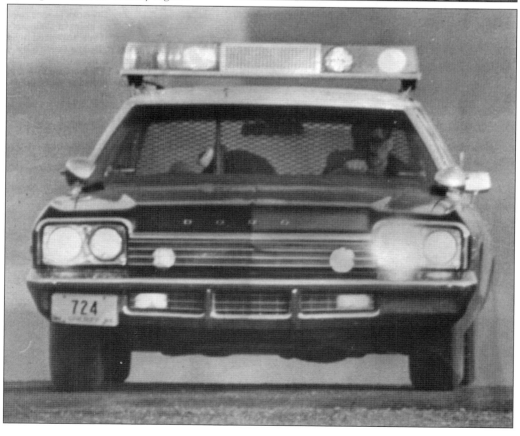

Between 1975 and 1978, the sheriff office's mobile operation center was painted black and white to match the patrol fleet's color pattern.

The sheriff's mobile operation center, pictured here around 1975–1978, served as a command post for special or emergency operation details.

Between 1975 and 1980, the sheriff's office's marked patrol vehicles donned the black-and-white color pattern. Pictured standing outside the vehicle is Deputy Terry Scanlon.

Deputy Ronald Klien is pictured here is the mid-1970s conducting a vehicle and traffic stop.

Sgt. Robert Leo, pictured here around 1979, stands alongside his marked patrol vehicle.

This photograph from about 1979 features the sheriff's crime scene search vehicle. Evidence technicians assigned to the criminalistics, crime lab unit, utilized this vehicle to respond to major crime scenes.

In 1978, the sheriff's office utilized the Chrysler Monaco model for its patrol fleet. These were equipped with the first of the area's law enforcement to install interior bulletproof plastic safety shields between the front and back seat compartments that could be opened and closed. Previous models were either wire mesh or rigid plastic barriers. In 1979, the sheriff's office scaled down to Chrysler Newports that sported a 360 engine.

This photograph, dated September 1, 1981, depicts a black-and-white Chrysler LeBaron patrol vehicle. This image illustrated the first seven-point star vehicle marking. This patrol vehicle sported a newly design light bar, air-conditioning, power windows, steering, and brakes.

The sheriff's office adopted a white and gold insignia vehicle color pattern between 1981 to 1994. Pictured here is a Dodge Diplomat.

By 1981, the sheriff's patrol vehicles were white with a gold seven-point star insignia. Deputy Lee Haynesworth is pictured standing next to his newly designed patrol car around 1981.

Several variations of gold striping were added during the late 1980s and early 1990s, as seen in this image from 1990.

In 1990, the sheriff's office adopted the Chevy Caprice for its patrol fleet. The vehicle color pattern was changed to black with gold and red highlights. The motto "Since 1794" was displayed vertically upon the rear fender.

In 1989, the office organized a crime-scene specialist unit and incorporated specialized trained and equipped evidence technicians with road patrol. These ET units utilized modified marked patrol vehicles, served as backup to patrol post units, and improved upon response time and attention to crime and vehicle crash scenes requiring evidence recovery work. Pictured here in 1994 is Deputy J. Anderson of ET 40.

Pictured here is a 1995 Onondaga County Sheriff's Office marked Chevy Caprice.

In 1994, the sheriff's office adopted a bus as a command post and personnel-transport vehicle.

By 2010, the sheriff's office moved to the Ford Crown Victoria to outfit its patrol fleet.

The *Peace Keeper* armed vehicle pictured here was retired in 2008.

In 2008, the *Bearcat* armored vehicle replaced the previous *Peace Keeper*.

By the late 1990s, the office utilized a versatile mobile command center for specialized and emergency operations.

In 2013, the sheriff's office adopted the Chevy Caprice.

The 2013 Chevy marked patrol vehicles maintained the black with gold and red highlights color pattern.

Pictured here is a close up view of the gold seven-point star insignia. The "Since 1794" banner was highlighted in red.

Pictured here in 1975 is an Onondaga County Sheriff snowmobile patrol unit.

This Onondaga County Sheriff snowmobile unit is pictured here in 1975. The snowmobiles were used for search and rescue, and special law enforcement details.

Around 1960, the sheriff's office introduced its first water patrol boat—the *Restless Lady*.

A water patrol boat is pictured here in Onondaga Lake in 1962.

By 1967, the water patrol boats became more specialized, as illustrated by this Thunderbird boat patrol. Pictured here are, from left to right, Blanchard Crysler, James Miraco, Michael Hanley, and Richard Pickard.

In 1970, the sheriff's boat patrols were utilized to police water-sporting events, water safety, and dive team recovery details.

Pictured here in 1978 are, from left to right, James Hickein, Undersheriff William Burns, William Stonecipher, and Lt. Anthony Valleriani.

In August 2001, the sheriff office's navigation unit retired a 1986 Boston Whaler and acquired two new boats: a 20-foot Marada and a 20-foot Seaswirl. The new boats augmented the unit's 24-foot Sportscraft and two jet ski watercrafts. Deputy Christopher Dell is pictured here in 2001 with the Seaswirl patrol boat.

The OSCO's helicopter aviation program, operation air stop (air-to-surface tactical offensive patrol), became operational in 1975. Initially it was a consolidated City of Syracuse Police Department and Onondaga County Sheriff's Office aviation program. Three Hiller OH-23D (1959 to 1963 vintage) helicopters outfitted the unit. The photograph is dated June 2, 1978.

Pictured here in 1977, the operation air stop helicopters were equipped with a public-address system and multifrequency radios for air-traffic control and police-agency communications. Normal flight height was 1,000 to 1,200 feet and lowered to 500 feet for situational response. Top air speed was 83 knots (96 miles per hour).

By 1977, the aviation program's potential was realized. Arrest rates increased, and crime rates dropped in areas where the helicopters were deployed with ground units. It proved effective in locating illegal marijuana fields and in responding to vehicle-pursuit situations. This image is dated 1976.

The air-stop Hiller helicopters were sometimes called "whirly birds, choppers, or chopper coppers." When the aviation program began, it was considered experimental. By 1979, the program had proven to be a versatile and effective crime-prevention and emergency-response service. The Hillers remained operational from 1975 to 1980.

In 1980, the city police department discontinued its involvement in the aviation-unit program. However, the sheriff's office continued its aviation unit and replaced the Hillers with the 206 Bell Jet Ranger turbine helicopter. This second-generation helicopter became commonly known as *Air One*. This ship was in service from 1980 to 1998.

Boasting improved equipment, increased passenger capacity, and expanded versatility in performance capability, the 206 ranger *Air One* served the collective municipal, law-enforcement, public-health, emergency medical–air medivac, and firefighting services.

In 1999, the sheriff office replaced the 206 ranger with a larger and more powerful 407 Bell Jet Ranger. This photograph illustrates these second (on the ground 206 ranger *Air One*) and third (airborne 407 ranger *Air One*) generation helicopters.

The Onondaga County Sheriff *Air One* 407 Bell Jet Ranger provided a multipurpose law-enforcement and emergency-service response. Capabilities included serving as an aerial observation platform, firefighting capabilities, search and rescue, and emergency medivac transport. The ship had a seven-passenger capability and was equipped with a night light source, a forward-looking infrared FLIR system, and a video camera system.

Pictured here are mid-1990s uniform items set with a 1928 photograph of uniformed Onondaga County deputies.

Five

PEOPLE, EVENTS, AND UNIFORMS

Since 1794, the deeds and character of the men and women of the Onondaga County Sheriff's Office have forged the right to boast a proud professional heritage. The echoes of that past are resounded throughout that heritage and invoke a sense of accomplishment, pride, purpose, and tradition. Celebrating that legacy ensures that those echoes will remain in the hopes, ambitions, ideals, dreams, and reputations of those who will follow in the wake. The following images serve to illustrate that enduring character.

On October 1, 1851, federal marshals attempted the arrest of escaped Missouri slave William "Jerry" Henry, a Syracuse resident, under the authority of the 1850 Fugitive Slave Law. A large abolitionist force responded, and a violent disturbance broke out. The Onondaga County Sheriff mobilized the local (artillery) militia to a dry-fire drill several blocks away and diverted the attention of the disturbance. Jerry made his escape from the federal marshals during the artillery show and escaped to freedom in Canada. The Jerry Rescue statue located in Syracuse, New York, commemorates the event.

During the mid-1800s, when the Erie Canal closed during the winter, hundreds of orphaned canal boys were abandoned and congregated in the streets of urban centers along the canal for shelter and survival. Absent other relief, jails served as an asylum for these wayward youth. In response, a reform movement pressed for the wellbeing of these "little colonies of waifs." Historically, the movement contributed to the beginnings of a juvenile-justice system in New York State. The Erie Canal boy and mule statue located in Syracuse is reminiscent of the episode.

Pictured here in 1901 are Sheriff Marvin (Seated second from left with pipe), Deputy Francis Cahill (standing left), and John Russell (standing far right). Deputies would not don uniforms until 1928.

This is the earliest recorded badge for the sheriff's office. The exact dates of its service are unknown. Although, it is known that the badge was in service in 1901. The badge was silver with black lettering. In 2000 and 2001, a sheriff's office adopted an optional bicentennial badge modeled after this 1901 pattern. The bicentennial badge was silver with a gold banner, and NYS seal highlights.

Prior to 1914, deputies were paid from revenues generated by civil process. In 1914, the position became a salaried post. Pictured here in 1913 are Onondaga County Sheriff deputies, identified by last name only, from left to right, Negg, Betzer, Hoffmier, Wright, Phillips, and Green.

In 1928, Deputy Sheriff Kenneth Parker escorted escaped Auburn Prison convict Jesse Thomas. In this photograph, Thomas is escorted with handcuffs and a chain-linked come-along device.

In 1928, Sheriff Michael O'Brien organized the office's first uniform patrol. Pictured here are, from left to right, (first row) Michael Piano, Lester Rawlings, Sylvester Eslick, and William Leonard; (second row) Thomas Cooper, Raymond Dear, Porter Baker, and Ernest Monica.

This badge was adopted by the sheriff's office's first road patrol in 1928. The exact date when it went out of service is unknown. The badge was silver with black lettering. The practice of placing numbers on badges was introduced by English Metropolitan Police in 1829.

COUNTY'S WOMEN SHERIFF CORPS COMPLETE

In 1926, Sheriff Lewis Scriber (pictured front center) organized the county's woman sheriff corps. The original toll listed 24 members, including the sheriff's wife. These women's division deputies served as matrons, juvenile officers, and dance-hall investigators.

Pictured here in 1936 are Michael Piano (kneeling far left), Lester Rawlings (kneeling 2nd right), and Raymond Dear (standing far right). The others are unidentified.

Records and folklore related to the sheriff's office peacekeeping role with the sovereign Onondaga Nation extend to 1794. Noted episodes of the sheriff's office involvement in confederacy feuds are recorded during the terms of Sheriff Thomas Munroe (1934–1937), Sheriff Patrick Corbett (1964–1978), and Sheriff John C. Dillon (1978–1994). These interactions have led to current practices and policies that encourage a continued peaceful cooperation between the Onondaga Nation and the Onondaga County Sheriff's Office. Deputy Raymond Dear is pictured here in 1939 with unidentified members of the Onondaga Nation.

From 1794 to 1846, the sheriff was an appointed post, selected by the governor. Between 1846 and 1937, the position was an elected post, limited to nonconsecutive four-year terms. In 1938, it became legal for a sheriff to be elected for consecutive terms. Deputy Sarto C. Major, who would later serve as sheriff of Onondaga County from 1959 to 1963, is pictured here around 1938.

This portrait of Deputy Harold F. Griebno from about 1936 is a classic image of the era. Illustrated is the weapon-retention lanyard attached to the cross-drawn revolver. The uniform patch radio patrol highlighted the new innovation of vehicle radio communication. Harold Griebno served 35 years (1929–1964). By 1954, Griebno had developed an emergency defense plan that became a model for sheriff's offices across the state, and transformed the agency's ledger record-filing system into a modern cross-indexed numerical system, still used today. In 2000, Griebno posthumously received the sheriff's office personal achievement award.

This badge, in gold with black lettering, is dated to the 1930s. Between 1947 and 1960, this badge was used to distinguish sergeant rank.

This image from about 1938 was recovered from the scrapbook of the late Deputy Raymond Dear (right). Deputy Dear and another unidentified deputy escort prisoner George Bedsworth from Auburn Prison to face escape charges in Syracuse.

Being that sheriffs did not maintain records between changing administrations, dating some early badge designs are approximation based on recovered photographs. In the mid-to-late 1930s, the sheriffs sported a gold shield badge. Prior to 1944, the sheriff's office adopted a silver badge that featured a brass New York State seal center. This image, recovered from a scrapbook, was undated is but likely from the 1930s or 1940s. Deputy Raymond Dear (wearing the 1930s-era badge) is inspecting the new 1940s-era badges.

The period for this era badge dates to the late 1930s or early 1940s. The badge was silver with a brass New York State seal center.

This image from the late 1940s or 1950s illustrates the classic motorcycle pantaloon jodhpurs, leather shin putts, and cross-drawn holster with safety lanyard. Pictured here are deputies Frank Rice (left) and Blanchard Crysler.

Dating images from badge patters is confusing and approximate. In this late-1950s image, Blanchard Crysler (right) is wearing a badge vintage 1944–1960. Sgt. John Checkowski (second from right) is wearing a 1936 vintage badge. The earlier vintage badge was worn by sergeants during this era to distinguish rank. The two individuals pictured to the left are unidentified.

This image, dated May 20, 1941, features Deputy Walter Foote.

Sergeant Beebe is pictured here donning a dark navy blue uniform with grey highlights. The sergeant stripes on the uniform date the image to sometime after 1947.

This image from the 1940s was recovered from the scrapbook of the late Deputy Bert Reardon. Deputy Reardon (left) is pictured with an unidentified deputy and an unidentified municipal police officer.

This 1947 staged photograph features Deputy Arthur Kasson in a classic winter uniform.

Prior to 1947, ranks were titled in hierarchy as deputy, third deputy, second deputy, and first deputy. In 1947, the sheriff's office adopted military titles to distinguish rank. This January 19, 1947, photograph illustrates Sheriff Robert G. Wasmer promoting deputies to the newly adopted rank of sergeant. Pictured here are, from left to right, Arthur Willis, Leo Beebe, Edward Dilligeant, and Sheriff Robert Wasmer.

The circumstance and individuals in this Cedar Street Jail photograph from the late 1940s are unidentified. The image is typical of an arrest photograph.

Special deputy Samuel E. Aupperle is pictured here in 1948. Special deputies have held a long traditional link to the office of sheriff, serving as an auxiliary reserve force, with roots that trace back to 450 to 650 CE during the English Anglo-Saxon period and the authority of the sheriff to summon the posse comitatus (power of the county). That authority was carried on by the common law legal traditions in England and the United States. Historical records reveal special deputies serving as early as 1928. Vintage badges depict special deputy insignia since about 1940.

Samuel E. Aupperle served as a special deputy from 1948 to 1956. The shield pictured featured a phoenix image on the top of the badge.

The uniform and badge pattern from this photograph is dated between 1944 and 1960. Pictured here around 1948 are, from left to right, Deputy Harold Griebno, Dewitt Cummings, William Hayford, Vick Tucci, and John "Chick" Checkowski.

The December 1948 date of this Cedar Street Jail photograph was identified by the calendar posted on the back wall. Pictured here from left to right are Arthur Willis, Dewitt Cummings, Joseph Kanasola, Victor Tucci, unidentified, William Hayford, Frank Rice, and Edward Diligent.

Although the exact adoption date of this pictured badge is unknown, the earliest recorded date for the badge was December 1944. The badge was gold with blue enamel highlights. The badge featured a phoenix image at its apex.

From left to right, Deputy Joseph Kanasola, Deputy Bert Reardon, and an unidentified deputy examine a stolen safe in this photograph dated February 12, 1949.

From left to right, arrestee Edwin Smith, Deputy Dewitt Cummings, and Deputy Frank Rice are pictured here on December 14, 1948.

The sergeant stripes pictured on the uniform to the right reveal a post-1947 image. This 1950s image features, from left to right, Harold Griebno, Robert Ashmore, Alex Cellie, and Leo Beebe. Sergeant Beebe also sports a 1930s vintage badge. The earlier vintage badges were issued to sergeants as a rank insignia.

Pictured here in the 1950s are an unidentified court deputy (left) and Deputy Alfred Antonello (right).

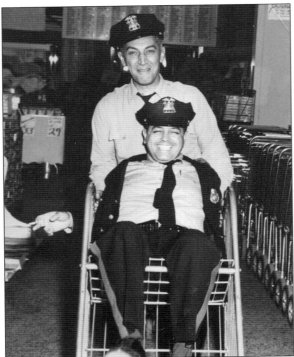

It has been said that all a good cop needs is common sense, a little compassion, and a sense of humor. Pictured here in the 1950s are deputies Alfred Antonello (back) and Joe Nicoletti (front) practicing that sense of humor while investigating a burglary scene at Williams Grocery Store, located at Route 11 and Taft Road in the town of Salina.

Pictured here from left to right are Sgt. Arthur Willis, an unidentified suspect, Deputy Dewitt Cummings, unidentified, and Deputy Frank Rice logging a booking at the Cedar Street Jail.

Pictured here examining a recovered knife at an unidentified crime scene in the 1950s are, from left to right, Deputy Fred Summers, Det. Dewitt Cummings, and Deputy Frank Rice.

This photograph from the 1950s was recovered from the scrapbook of Deputy Dominick Tedesco (pictured).

Pictured here in the 1950s is Sgt. Bert Reardon. During this era, there was no official distinction between deputies assigned to the jail or patrol duties. Deputies were assigned to watch assignment according to need.

Deputies Bert Reardon (left) and James Bateman are pictured here in the 1950s.

On February 27, 1950, Det. Dewitt Cummings (left) and Deputy Frank Rice escort two unidentified Yates Hotel holdup suspects.

Pictured here in January 1951 are, from left to right, Deputy Andy Hoffman and Capt. Blanchard Crysler. Captain Crysler shared advice with new recruits, particularly what he referred to as the three Bs that will land officers in trouble—booze, broads, and bribes.

This photograph is dated April 8, 1951, and features police dispatch–radio operator Deputy Francis Martin. Early mobile police-radio systems operated in conjunction with telephone pole–mounted police call boxes. As radio developments improved, police dispatch–radio systems remained agency independent until 1964. In 1964, Sheriff Corbett introduced the countywide "Onondaga Law Enforcement Mobile Radio District" (OLMRD) police radio system. The success of this improved radio communication system paved the way for the (1992) 911 Emergency Communication System.

Pictured on April 7, 1952, are, from left to right, Deputy Andy Hoffman, Deputy Henry Coughlin, and arrestees Raymond Bailey and Philip Freeman.

Pictured here on March 5, 1953, are, from left to right, Det. John Joy and suspect Rev. George Hetenyi. The reverend is being escorted after his conviction for murder in the second degree.

This image from the 1950s captures the bite of winter accident scenes. Pictured on the left is Blanchard Crysler. The others in the photograph are unidentified.

In May 1953, General Electric Corp. employees went on strike at the Electronics Parkway plant in the town of Salina. The strike became heated when a scab goon drove through the picket lines, injuring strikers.

This photograph is dated January 23, 1954. Pictured here are, from left to right, Sgt. Leo Beebe, Deputy Jim Bateman, Deputy Victor Tucci, and Deputy Henry Caughlin.

This 1955 photograph features Deputy Henry Caughlin at the Pierce Grocery Store, located on the Onondaga Nation Reservation Territory. The other individuals in the photograph are unidentified.

This photograph is dated November 30, 1955.

On January 26, 1958, Deputy Alfred Antonello investigated an accident scene on Route 298 at the Thruway Bridge.

On August 31, 1958, new school-zone safety posters were posted. Captured in the photograph are, from left to right, Harry LaVier (executive secretary of the Automobile Club of Syracuse), Deputy Leonard Crane, and Sheriff Albert Stone.

This photograph illustrates the 1960 adoption of the six-point star badge. The only deputy identified in this photograph is James Wolf (second from left).

The six-point star badge was adopted by sheriff departments across New York State in order to distinguish sheriff departments from police departments. The collective effort was intended to recognize the civil and jail components of the office of sheriff. The Onondaga County badge was gold with a blue enamel NYS seal highlight.

In March 1960, Carrier Corporation employees went on strike at the Thompson Road plant in the town of Dewitt. Pictured above on March 30, 1960, are an unidentified striker arrestee (right) and Sgt. Blanchard Crysler (left).

In 1960, General Electric employees went on strike at the Electronics Parkway plant in the town of Salina. The strike became heated as picketers attempted to block the entranceways to the plant.

This radio dispatch photograph is dated December 26, 1961. Pictured here are Sgt. Blanchard Crysler and unidentified deputy.

This photograph from the 1960s features an unidentified sergeant at dispatch duty.

This photograph of Deputy Robert Datlo at the Cedar Street Jail is dated March 17, 1963.

In 1963, Sheriff Sarto C. Major, a number of sheriff deputies, the superintendent, and several staff at the Jamesville Penitentiary were named on indictments related to the failure to segregate youthful offenders from adult prisoners at the county jail facilities. However, the evidence established the inadequacy of the jail facilities and the physical inability to accommodate segregation requirements. The charges were subsequently dropped on the night of the 1963 sheriff election. Sheriff Major lost the election to Sheriff Patrick C. Corbett. This 1963 photograph features Deputy Joseph Kanasola at the county courthouse.

This June 1964 photograph shows Deputy Bartosiewotz (left) and Sheriff Patrick Corbett (right) operating the sheriff's office first traffic-radar unit.

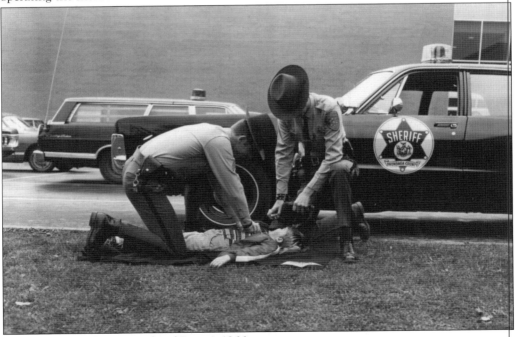

This promotional image is dated June 4, 1966.

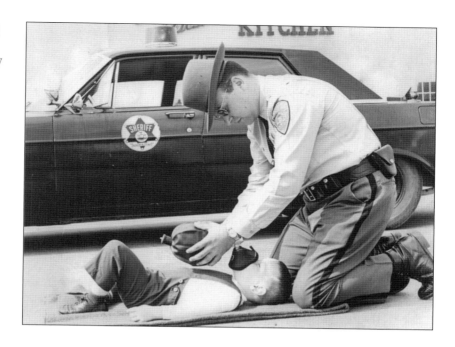

On April 30, 1966, Sgt. Thomas Lavere escorted entertainer Bob Hope on a visit to Syracuse.

This honor guard photograph is dated May 1966. Pictured here are, from left to right, Deputies Anguoi, Stevenson, Kerwin, and Hilber.

This August 8, 1966, Onondaga Lake Parkway photograph depicts the sheriff's office posting signs announcing a new telephone number. A new Centrex system changed all telephone numbers in county buildings. Pictured here are Capt. Blanchard Crysler and George Millard, senior communications consultant for the telephone company.

This winter 1966 photograph captures a familiar Onondaga County scene.

On August 29, 1967, Deputy Monty Euston escorted Robert Kennedy on a visit to Syracuse.

On April 19, 1969, Lt. Robert Mekkelsen and Deputy L. Pickard examine a .30-caliber rifle recovered from a King's Park Apartment sniper suspect.

Pictured in this 1970s roll call are, from left to right, John Dwyer, Terry Scanlon, Dwayne Lalond, unidentified (Hat down), Lt. Leo Capria (back toward camera), William Altenburg, R. Nardone, Richard Cox, unidentified (partially visible), Terry Freel, R. Delia, Allan Sickman, and Sgt. James Thornton.

This early 1970s photograph neatly depicts the dress uniform of the era. Pictured here from left to right are unidentified, Lt. James Donovan, Thomas Metz, and Daniel Patk.

Deputy Christopher Richards is pictured in this 1970s image conducting a vehicle and traffic stop.

Deputy Bill Lynn is pictured here around 1973–1974 donning the dress uniform of the era.

This 1973 or 1974 vintage photograph features from left to right deputies Bill Lynn, Charles Florczyk, Daniel Patk, and Gerry Solan.

In 1975, a disturbance broke out at the Jamesville Penitentiary facility. Sheriff Corbett mobilized the sheriff department to put down the disturbance. Crowd-control details made up of department members trained as an occurrence control unit.

This "Call the Sheriff" promotional image from about 1975 was featured in a Deputy Sheriff Benevolent Association circulation.

In 1974, jail matron Elsie Klocek (pictured here in 1969) won a discrimination complaint against the county contending that matrons were discriminated against by being paid less than their male counterparts. The State Human Rights Commission and the State Supreme Court Appellate Division ruled in favor of the complaint. Subsequently, the matron position was abolished, and female deputies earned equal pay and title as deputy within the sheriff's office.

The six-point matron badge was adopted in 1960. The badge became obsolete when the matron title was abolished in 1974.

In 1979, the sheriff's office began a K-9 unit to augment its law-enforcement capabilities and service. Pictured here in 1979 are Deputy Paul Carey and his K-9 partner Shamus.

As illustrated in this 1979 image (Deputy Paul Carey and Shamus), patrol cars were adapted and marked for specific K-9 use.

A K-9 unit employs rigorous training. The mutual trust resulting from the training makes it possible to apply the dog's natural abilities to police-service work. Deputy Paul Carey and Shamus are pictured here in 1980 training.

The early K-9 program developed with recognizable success. Eventually, the K-9 teams would develop to perform a multitude of tasks, including building and area searches, tracks, explosive-device searches, criminal apprehensions, drug searches, and person-crowd control. Pictured here from left to right are Paul Carey, Dwayne Lalond, and John Dwyer.

Throughout his career, Sgt. Jeff Gates (pictured here around 1985 with Shamus) distinguished himself as a K-9 trainer and handler.

Shamus holds the distinct honor as the sheriff's office first K-9 partner.

By the mid-1980s, the K-9 unit was well established within the Onondaga County Sheriff's Office operation under the auspices of the patrol division.

Each of the K-9 unit dogs possess and demonstrate distinct personality characteristics. The dog candidates are subjected to an evaluation process to determine suitability. Pictured here are, from left to right, Saber, Shamus, and Magnum.

In 1980, the sheriff's office adopted the seven-point star badge for its police division as an esprit de corps initiative. Sheriff John Dillon (in suite) is pictured here presenting the seven-point star badge to police-division deputies. The uniform patch still illustrated the six-point star patch. The six-point star image was adopted among sheriff's offices across New York State in 1960 to recognize the sheriff's diversity in serving jail- and civil-policing responsibilities. The seven-point star patch was adopted by 1989.

In 1980, the sheriff department's police division adopted the seven-point star badge. By 1989, the seven-point badge would be adopted by the jail and civil divisions. The Onondaga County badge was gold with black enamel highlights.

Pictured here in 1980 are, from left to right, Daniel Ptak, Lt. James Thornton, and Terry Freel. At the time that the photograph was taken, the campaign-style Stetson was a trial issue. The trooper-style Stetson with three dimples replaced this cover.

This 1984 SWAT member photograph features, from left to right, (first row) Joseph Snell, Donald Stewart, Mark Doneburg, Paul Carey, and Harry Homer; (second row) Thomas Paglia, Alex Romanenko, Michael Haven, Lenny Richer, George Christy, Edward Higgins, Allen Sickmon, Joseph Mehlek, John Scarson, Donald Evans, and Walter Blake.

Pictured here around 1985 are, from left to right, Sgt. Michael Haven, 1st Sgt. Thomas Paglia, Capt. David Stevenson, Maj. Joseph Mehlek, and Undersheriff Robert Burns.

This 1985 photograph features Sheriff John C. Dillon at the St. Patrick's Day Parade.

It has been a long-standing practice for the members of the sheriff's office to participate in the St. Patrick's Day parade. This 1995 image features Sheriff Kevin E. Walsh (front center) in a group photograph of the St. Patrick's Day parade detail.

Discover Thousands of Local History Books
Featuring Millions of Vintage Images

Arcadia Publishing, the leading local history publisher in the United States, is committed to making history accessible and meaningful through publishing books that celebrate and preserve the heritage of America's people and places.

Find more books like this at
www.arcadiapublishing.com

Search for your hometown history, your old stomping grounds, and even your favorite sports team.